GW00728019

THE HAMMER & SICKLE IS THE NUMBER OF THE BEAST

A short version of THE HAMMER & SICKLE IS THE MARK OF THE BEAST

NICHOLAS BRAND

White Stone Publishing

Typeset and designed by Nicholas Brand

White Stone Publishing: njcbrand@hotmail.co.uk

ISBN: 9798322268000

Revised 9.1.25

Unless otherwise indicated all scripture quotations are from The Holy Bible, the Revised Standard Version or the New Revised Standard Version.

THE HEBREW/GREEK ALPHABETICAL NUMBER SYSTEM

1	Αα	alpha	א	aleph
2	Ββ	beta	ב	bet
3	Γγ	gamma	ג	gimel
4	Δδ	delta	ד	dalet
5	Εε	epsilon	ה	he
6	Ϛϛ	digamma	ו	vav
7	Ζζ	zeta	ז	zayin
8	Ηη	eta	ח	chet
9	Θθ	theta	ט	tet
10	Ιι	iota	י	yod
20	Κκ	kappa	כ	kaf
30	Λλ	lamda	ל	lamed
40	Μμ	mu	מ	mem
50	Νν	nu	נ	nun
60	Ξξ	xi	ס	samekh
70	Οο	omicron	ע	ayin
80	Ππ	pi	פ	pey
90	Ϙϙ	koppa	צ	tzade
100	Ρρ	rho	ק	qof
200	Σσ	sigma	ר	resh
300	Ττ	tau	ש	s(h)in
400	Υυ	upsilon	ת	tav
500	Φφ	phi	תק	
600	Χχ	chi	תר	
700	Ψψ	psi	תש	
800	Ωω	omega	תת	
900	Ͳͳ	san	תתק	

CONTENTS

HEBREW/GREEK-ENGLISH TRANSLITERATION

χι ϛ (chi, iota, digamma = 616)	ChIV
תרטז (tav, resh, tet, zayin = 616)	TRTZ
תריו (tav, resh, yod, vav = 616)	TRIW
תריון (tav, resh, yod, vav, nun = therion)	TRIWN
תרסו (tav, resh, samekh, vav = 666)	TRSW

1

INTRODUCTION

**. . . . the mark of the name of the beast or the number of the
name of the beast. (Rev. 13:17)**

The Hammer & Sickle is the mark of the Beast. It represents both
the name of the Beast and the number of the name of the Beast.

The number of the Beast is the numerical value of the Hebrew
letters derived from the transliteration of the Greek word θηριον.
This number is 616, not 666.

The Hammer & Sickle mark incorporate all the criteria of Rev.
13:17-18. It is:

- a rebus (*charagma*) representing the name of the Beast (which
  is "beast": θηριον, in Greek).
- the number of the name of the Beast (616) in the form of monograms, both in Greek and Hebrew letters.
- The various elements of the Hammer & Sickle, through their
  acrophonic meaning, signify the number 616: tav (400) =
  "mark", resh (200) = "head", yod (10) = "handle", and vav (6)
  = "hook".

2

THE MARK OF THE NAME OF THE BEAST

The Hammer & Sickle is a rebus which signifies the word Therion ("beast" in Greek)

> . . . .the mark of the name of the beast or the number of its name. (Rev. 13:18)

The Hammer & Sickle can be perceived as a rebus signifying the name "Therion", θηριον ("Beast" in Greek). A rebus is a puzzle consisting of pictures representing syllables and words.

In the Soviet emblem, the sickle is depicted on top of the hammer. Visually, this is highly significant. It indicates that the letters that form the word for "hammer" in the word for "sickle" should be "crossed out". The letters that remain spell the hidden word. This word is "beast" (θηριον).

There are several Greek words for "sickle": *drepanon, zanklon, theristron, harpe* and only two common Greek words for "hammer": *sphura* and *raister*. The word *raister* (ραιστηρ, "hammer") indicates that *theristron* (θεριστρον) is the intended word for "sickle" because the letters which spell *raister* ("hammer") form the central part of *theristron*: *ther-ristr-on*.

The Greek for "Red Star", ερυθρος αστηρ (*eruthros aster*), might also point to *theristron* given how many letters they have in common.

As explained before, visually, the sickle appears to "cross out" the hammer. Having removed the letters *-ristr-* from *theristron*, the word for "beast" can be perceived: *therion*.

The diagram of the Hammer & Sickle below illustrates how the sickle crosses over the hammer on the Soviet emblem.

The Hammer & Sickle represents the union of the workers and the peasants. Likewise, the words for "sickle" (*theristron*) and "hammer" (*raister*) are united in the word *theristron*. However, rather than just seeing a union of the words for "hammer" and "sickle", one must also perceive that the sickle, by crossing over the hammer, is "striking out" the letters which spell the word "hammer" in Greek to unveil the word *therion*.

THERISTRON - RAISTER = THERION

3

THE MARK OF THE NUMBER OF THE NAME

OF THE BEAST

The two forms of 616 in Hebrew letters

The number 16 is formed using the substitute letters tet (9) and zayin (7) instead of yod (10) and vav (6) for religious reasons.

Consequently, the number 616 is invariably constructed with the Hebrew letters tav (400), resh (200), tet (9), and zayin (7) instead of the expected tav, resh, yod, and vav.

Acrophony

The Hammer & Sickle should be perceived as a pictogram based on acrophony.

The names of the letters of the Hebrew and Greek alphabet are related to each other. For example, the name of the first three letters of the Hebrew alphabet, *alpha, beta, gamma* are similar to the names of the first three letters of the Hebrew alphabet: *aleph, bet,* and *gimmel.* Most of the letters of these two alphabets share similar names because most of their letters are derived from the same source.

The letters of the alphabet were named after things the names of which began with the sound of that particular letter of the alphabet. This system is called acrophony. For example, the Hebrew letter *bet* means "house"; *dalet* means "house", and so on. The names of the Greek letters *beta* and *delta* share the same derivation as these two Hebrew letters.

The Hammer & Sickle depicts the name Therion ("beast") through acrophony

...the mark of the name of the beast ... (Rev. 13:17)

The Hebrew letter *tav* means "mark"; the letter *resh* is derived from a word which means "head"; *yad* means "hand", but can also mean "handle"; *vav* means "hook".

The Hammer Sickle is clearly a mark. The mark itself signifies the letter *tav.* Admittedly, any mark would serve to represent the letter *tav. Tav* is the Hebrew word found in Ezekiel for the "mark" that is put on the foreheads of those who sigh and groan over all the abominations committed in Jerusalem (Ezek. 9:4).

The "head" of the hammer serves to represent the letter *resh*; the handle of the hammer represents the letter *yod*; the "sickle" represents the letter *vav* because the sickle has the shape of a hook (and sickles are called "reaping-hooks").

The Hammer & Sickle represents the letters *tav, resh, yod,* and *vav* diagramatically. Transliterated into Greek letters, these

Hebrew letters signify the Greek name "beast", *therio(n)*: θηριο(ν) = תריו. (See Fig. 1 page 7.)

These Hebrew letters also signify the number 616 in Hebrew (400+200+10+6). However these letters are now invariably replaced with תרטז (400+200+9+7) to avoid the combination of the letters yod(10) and vav (6) which is associated with the holy name of God.

The acrophonic symbols (mark, head, handle, hook) signify the name of the Beast

The letters tav ת, resh ר, yod י and vav ו signify the NAME of the Beast, because, when transliterated into Greek letters, they spell the name of the Beast, which is *therion* ("beast"). These letters also signify the number 616, hence the number of the name of the Beast is 616.

The alternative letters for 616, tav, resh, tet, and zayin, signify the NUMBER OF THE NAME of the Beast (because 616 = *therion*).

The transliteration of the letters that spell the word for "beast" in Aramaic or Greek result in the number 616 in the other language. They do not transliterate into the word for "beast" since the resultant letters do not spell "beast" in the letters of that particular language.

Monograms: the number of the name of the Beast

. . . or the number of the name of the beast . . . (Rev. 13:17,
author's translation based on text of Codex Ephraemi Rescriptus)

The Hammer and Sickle can be perceived as a monogram as well as a pictogram based on acrophony .

The Hammer and Sickle can be perceived as a monogram of the number 616 in Greek letters χις (=616) in reverse and Hebrew letters תרטז (TRTZ = 616) in obverse.

The variant reading 616 is not yet found in the main text of any modern version of the Bible, but is acknowledged in a footnote in over half of the most important editions of the Bible. The most important witness to the number 616 is found in the *Codex Ephraemi Rescriptus*, where the number 616 is written out in full (*hexakosioi deka hex*).

Greek word for "600" in feminine plural (*hexakosiai*) agreeing with "Beast" in Aramaic (cheivah)

Two of the three great uncials have the Greek word for "six hundred" (*hexakosiai*) in the feminine plural. None of the Greek words in Rev. 13:18 with which this word can possibly agree is feminine. Therefore the only reasonable explanation for this choice of gender is that the word agrees with the Aramaic word for "beast", *cheivah*, which is a feminine noun.

Failure to realize this connection with *cheivah* probably accounts for why later copies have the word for "six hundred" in either the masculine or neuter plural. These copies were either made from manuscripts that had the number using the numerical alphabet system or were deliberately changed to agree with one of the Greek words in Rev. 13:18.

The number of the name of the Beast: (Fig. 1, acrophony); (Figs. 2 & 3, monograms)

VAV = "HOOK"   YOD = "HANDLE"   RESH = "HEAD"   TAV = "MARK"

תריו=THERION

ZAYIN   TET   RESH   TAV

תרטז=616

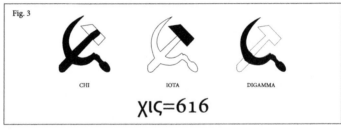

CHI   IOTA   DIGAMMA

ΧΙϚ=616

The Greek letters fit the Hammer and Sickle

The transliterated Greek letters χις (616) equate to חיו, the core letters of the Aramaic word for "beast" חיוה. The Aramaic for "beast" is חיוה *cheyvah*. The word *cheyvah* is used many times in chapter 7 of the Book of Daniel, the chapter which prophesies the advent of the Beast.

The Old Testament is written mainly in Hebrew, but parts of Daniel (Dan. 2:4b-7:28) and parts of Ezra (Ezra 4:8-24; 5; 6:1-18; 7:12-26) are written in Aramaic.

The apocalypse of John was written down in classical Greek and the ancient Greek number system was based on the alphabet.

The Hammer and Sickle is the number of the Beast, a monogram of the Hebrew letters TRTZ (in obverse), which number 616, and of the three Greek letters which number 616 (in reverse).

The Greek letters χις serve as numbers in the Greek number system and total 616, because χ (chi) =600, ι (iota)=10, and ς (digamma)=6.

4

THE SEVEN KINGS OF THE BEAST

The seven heads are the seven "kings" of the former Soviet Union

The Beast's head represents "mountains" and "kings". The word "kings" signifies both "kingdoms" and "kings". The seven"kings" of the Soviet Union were:

1 Lenin
2 Joseph Stalin
3 Nikita Khrushchev
4 Leonid Brezhnev
5 Yuri Andropov
6 Konstantin Chernenko
7 Mikhail Gorbachev

The Beast, at his advent, will be the eighth "king", although his kingdom will be a restoration of the seventh kingdom (Rev. 17:11).

The Workers' and Peasants' Government

The formula "workers' and farmers' government" indicated the need for the workers to break with all traditional parties of the bourgeoisie in order, jointly with the farmers, to establish their own power.

Article 6 of the 1918 Constitution of the Russian Federated Soviet Republic exhibits the first state emblem of Soviet Russian. It consists of a Hammer & Sickle before a kind of shield with the sun at the bottom of it, but no Red Star above it.

The Hammer & Sickle represent the workers and peasants respectively.

The Soviet Union will be restored

The Beast, the fourth beast with iron teeth that Daniel saw rising out of the sea (Dan. 7:7), "was" and "it to come". The mortal wound of one of the Beast's heads signifies the collapse of the former USSR. Its healing signifies the restoration of the USSR. This restoration is imminent.

Soviet emblem is the mark of the Beast

And I saw a beast rising out of the sea, with ten horns ... (Rev. 13:1)

The USSR can be identified as the Beast through the Hammer & Sickle, its emblem, because the Hammer and Sickle is the mark of the Beast.

The Workers' and Peasants' Government incorporated the

Hammer & Sickle in its emblem in the 1918 Constitution of the RSFSR. The adoption of the Hammer & Sickle as the official emblem of the USSR happened during the third session of the Executive Committee of the USSR on 12 November 1923.

Each Soviet Socialist Republic (SSR) had its own emblem adorned with the Hammer & Sickle, thereby identifying them with the Beast.

The former USSR and the future USSR (the Beast and Ten Kings) comprise the Fourth Kingdom

And the ten horns that you saw are ten kings who have not yet received a kingdom, but they are to receive authority as kings for one hour, together with the beast. (Rev. 17:12)

During the seventh kingdom, the USSR, the Soviet Republics were not independent states but were merged within a union of Soviet Republics.

The Beast Kingdom, will will again be a union comprised of the Beast himself and ten of the former Soviet Republics (the Ten Kings). These states which will hand over their authority to the Beast being of one mind with the Beast.

The Little Horn (Dan. 7:8) is the Russian Federation. The other former Soviet Republics are the Ten Horns. The Russian Federation will uproot three former Soviet Republics before restoring the Soviet Union.

The seven heads of the Beast represent a succession of empires. The USSR is represented by the seventh head of the seven-headed Beast. The seven heads also represent the seven leaders (General Secretaries) of the Sovit Union.

At his advent, the Beast (the son of Perdition) will be the eighth leader of the Soviet Union. He is represented by the Beast itself.

The Ten Kings are represented by the horns of the Beast itself. The Beast and the Ten Kings shall reign for "one hour".

The eyes and mouth of the Little Horn indicate one man, the Son of Perdition. He will be the last ruler in this line of "kings" who have hegemony over the other Ten Horns. The line, or succession, of "kings" of the Little Horn runs from Vladimir Putin (and Boris Yeltsin) through to the Son of Perdition himself.

Russia-Ukraine war

I was considering the horns, when another horn appeared, a little one coming up among them; to make room for it three of the earlier horns were plucked up by the roots. (Dan. 7:8)

The Russian Federation will uproot three former Soviet Republics (Dan. 7:8; 7:24) before restoring the Soviet Union:

As for the ten horns, out of this kingdom ten kings shall arise, and another shall arise after them. This one shall be different from the former ones, and shall put down three kings. (Dan. 7:24)

As things stand today, it looks like Ukraine will be the first Horn to be uprooted. It would be pure speculation to try and predict which of the other Horns will be uprooted. Some military experts are already predicting that Moldova and Georgia (already invaded in 2008) might be the next countries to be invaded by Russia. The Russian Federation is trying to keep all the former Soviet Republics within its sphere of influence. Any CIS state which leans towards NATO is is danger of being invaded. The fact that the Ten Kings and the Beast will only be kings for one hour (Rev. 17:24) indicates that as soon as these three former Soviet Republics are uprooted, the Soviet Union will be restored shortly afterwards. The Commonwealth of Independent States will not endure for much longer before the restoration of the Soviet Union.

Restoration of the Soviet Union

. . . but its mortal wound was healed, and the whole earth followed the beast with wonder. (Rev. 13:3)

The Soviet Union will be restored to become the eighth kingdom. This restoration is described in Revelation in terms of a mortal wound being healed, a sword wound (Rev. 13:14).

The reference to a sword refers to the Cold War, which appeared to end with the apparent death of communism in the early 1990s. All the previous kingdoms that are represented by the heads of the Beast came to an end through defeat in war. The USSR appeared to have ended in a similar way, with many in the West gloating that they had won the Cold War (which Stalin termed the Third Word War).

The head wound (Rev. 13: 3) refers to the end of the Cold War, not the assassination of any individual. Its healing refers to the restoration of the Soviet Union when the Ten Kings hand over their sovereign power to the Beast himself.

5

THE SEVEN KINGDOMS OF THE BEAST

The seven kingdoms of the Beast

There are seven heads and seven kingdoms. The seventh head has a mortal wound which heals. The seven kingdoms are the following:

1. Neo-Babylonian Empire [625-539 BC]
2. Medes and Persians [539-330 BC]
3. Alexander the Great [332-323]/kingdom of Macedonia [306-168 BC]
4. Seleucids/kingdom of Syria [312-63 BC]
5. Ptolemies/kingdom of Egypt [305-30 BC]
6. Roman Republic/Empire [133 BC-1453]/ Ottoman Empire [1453-1922]
7. USSR [1922-1991]: the Beast that "was" and the future restored USSR: the Beast that is yet "to come"

The Table on the following page illustrates how the succession of these kingdoms is portrayed in the Book of Daniel in the form of the vision of the Statue and the various beasts seen in Daniel's and King Nebuchadnezzar's visions.

HEAD	BEAST	KINGDOM	NATION	STATUE	NOTES
1	Lion	Babylon	CHESED	Gold (head)	"five of whom have fallen" (Rev. 17:10)
2	Bear	Medo-Persian	MADAI/ PARAS	Silver (upper body)	
3	Leopard	Macedonia	JAVAN	Bronze (thigh and upper legs)	
4		Syria			
5		Egypt			
6		Roman/ Ottoman			"one is" (Rev. 17:10)
7	Fourth Beast	USSR (beast that "was"	MAGOG	Iron (lower legs)	"remain only a little while" (Rev. 17:10)
The Beast itself (Rev. 17:8)		USSR restored (Beast that "is to come"		Iron and clay (feet)	Little Horn (Dan. 7:8) and Ten Horns

The Chaldeans descended from Chesed (Gen. 22:22)

The Chaldeans (Hebrew: *chasdim*) ruled over the first of the seven-empires, the Babylonian Empire. They are descended from Chesed, one of the sons of Nahor, Abraham's brother (Gen. 22:22).

Daniel had a series of visions, each new vision building upon the previous one, to reveal the identities of the Four Kingdoms that will rule over the earth in succession.

The seven kingdoms are divided between four Kingdoms (or "World Kingdoms" in Keil's terminology) represented by the Lion, Bear, Leopard and Fourth Beast in Daniel's vision, with each beast representing different nations.

The Beast itself represents an eighth kingdom and a king. The king who fights the Lamb at Armageddon is the Beast, the Son of Perdition.

Many commentators mistakenly interpret the phrase "five of whom have fallen" to signify a succession of Roman emperors and are invariably unable to match any line of emperors to the seven heads in a convincing way.

The fact that the feet and mouth are distinguished from the other parts of the Beast's body indicates that the Beast represents the Little Horn, for in a similar way its "mouth" and "eyes" were distinguished from the other parts of its body.

The interpretation of "kings" as kingdoms is also supported by the fact that the Greek word for "fallen" (*epesen*) is the same Greek word that is used in describing the fall of the great city Babylon the Great herself in the very next chapter:

"Fallen, fallen (*epesen*) is Babylon the great! (Rev. 18:2).

As many commentators have noted, the word *epesen* is not an appropriate word to describe the end of an individual king.

The interchangeability of "kings" for "kingdoms" is also made explicit in verses Dan. 7:17 and Dan. 7:23: 'These four great beasts are four kings who shall arise out of the earth' (Dan. 7:17)

Satanic nature of all seven kingdoms

> **And another portent appeared in heaven; behold, a great red dragon, with seven heads and ten horns, and seven diadems upon his heads. (Rev. 12:3)**

The satanic nature of these seven kingdoms are revealed by the portent in the prophecy of the great Red Dragon (Rev. 12:3).

The Ten Horns

Represented by the toes of the Statue in Nebuchadnezzar's dream, these "kings" need not number exactly ten. This Statue also represents the Beast Man (the Son of Perdition), and hence the Little Horn of the Fourth Kingdom.

The Ten Horns do not represent the Soviet Republics themselves, but instead represent the independent states that arose from them after the collapse of the Soviet Union.

The Little Horn, the Russian Federation, is represented by the Beast itself. Its eyes and mouth represent the Son of Perdition himself.

The Ten Horns comprise of some, or all, of the following:

- Azerrbaijan
- Belarus
- Kazakhstan
- Kyrgyzstan
- Armenia
- Moldova
- Tajikstan
- Uzbekistan
- Turkmenistan

- Ukraine
- Lithuania
- Latvia
- Estonia
- Georgia

Daniel's visions of the Four Kingdoms

The Statue

Daniel's first vision enabled him to interpret King Nebuchadnez-zar's dream of the metallic image of a Statue of a man. The gold head represented King Nebuchadnezzar's kingdom, according to Daniel's interpretation of the dream, and hence the Babylonian Empire. The lower parts of the body represented successive empires.

The Statue represents the same succession of empires as the heads of the Beast. Like the Beast, the Statue also represents the Son of Perdition himself.

Four beasts rising from the sea

After this Daniel dreamed of four beasts rising from the sea: a Lion, a Bear, a Leopard, and a fearsome Fourth Beast with iron teeth and Ten Horns. The Leopard has four heads, the other beasts have only one head. These seven heads are represented by the seven heads of the Beast (Rev. 13:1). It can be inferred from the previous vision of the Statue that the first beast, the Lion, represents the Babylonian Empire. Like the Beast of Revelation, Daniel's Fourth Beast has ten horns.

The Ram and He-goat

The third vision was of a Ram (with two horns) being trampled on by a He-goat. The interpreting angel tells us that the large horn from which spring out four more is the King of Greece, and that the Ram with two horns represents the kings of Media and Persia. From this vision we can infer that the Bear of the previous vision was therefore the Medo-Persian Empire, and that the Leopard represents the four subsequent Javanic (Greek) empires.

The two horns of the Ram indicate two kingdoms, but is represented by only one of the heads of the Beast because the Medo-Persian Empire was a united kingdom. The two horns of the Ram, are a type for the ten horns of the Beast.

Further confirmation that the He-goat (Greece) represents the same nation as the Leopard is found in the repetition of the number four in the description of both the Leopard and the He-goat. As the leopard of the earlier vision has four heads and four wings, so the four horns which take the place of the he-goat's broken horn reach to the four winds of heaven. The four wings of the Leopard represent the four winds of heaven: "**there came up four conspicuous horns toward the four winds of heaven**" (Dan. 8:8).

Rome is a Javanic kingdom

Rome counts as one of the four horns of the He-Goat, because the Romans are descendants of Javan. The Romans are thus not the Fourth Kingdom as is widely believed, but belong to the Third Beast (the Leopard).

The Romans count as Javanic (Greek), because they are descendants of Kittim, a son of Javan (Gen. 10:4-5). Javan was a descendant of Japheth, one of the three sons of Noah. Javan's sons are listed in Genesis, one of whom was Kittim:

The sons of Javan: Elishah, Tarshish, Kittim, and Dodanim. From these the coastland peoples spread. (Gen. 10:4-5)

The Jewish commentator Ibn Ezra considered that Rome should

be included in the Third Kingdom on the grounds that they were related to the Greeks.

Kittim was a settlement in present-day Larnaca on the west coast of Cyprus, known in ancient times as Kition, or (in Latin) Citium. On this basis, the whole island became known as "Kittim" in Hebrew, including the Tanach, the Hebrew Bible. The name Kittim was often applied to all the Aegean islands and even to the West in general, especially the seafaring West.

The expression "isles of Kittim" (Jer. 2:10; Ezek. 27:6) indicates that this designation had already become a general descriptor for the Mediterranean islands long before the time of Josephus. Sometimes this designation was further extended to apply to Romans, Macedonians or Seleucid Greeks. For example, the beginning of 1 Maccabees that "Alexander the Great the Macedonian" had come from the "land of Kittim" (1 Macc. 1:1).

The Romans are considered to be the Kittim mentioned in Numbers 24:24. The mediaeval rabbinic compilation Yosippon contains a detailed account of the Kittim who are correlated to the Romans.

The Romans themselves believed that their ancestors originated from Anatolia (an area of Javan), fleeing with Aeneas from Troy, a legend told in Virgil's Aeneid. The Javanic nature of the Roman Empire is quite apparent from the fact that Justinian was the last Roman emperor to speak Latin. From his reign onwards all the Roman emperors spoke Greek.

The Javanic nature of the Roman Empire is also apparent from the fact that the new Roman capital, Constantinople, is situated at the mouth to the Ionian Sea, a sea which derives its name from Javan.

The Roman Empire is the sixth kingdom: "one is" (Rev. 17:10)

> **. . . they are also seven kings, five of whom have fallen, one is . . . (Rev 17:10)**

The interpreting angel tells John that one of the heads "**is**" and that "**five have fallen**". (Rev. 17: 10). The one that "is" can only be the Roman Empire, the empire prevalent at the time of John's prophecy.

The identification of Rome as the sixth head rules out any possibility that Rome is the Fourth Kingdom, for if one allocates the first two heads of the Beast to the Lion and the Bear respectively, the sixth head must by any reckoning be one of the four heads of the Leopard.

Even if one were to allocate two heads of the Beast to the Medo-Persian Empire (the Bear), Rome would still have to be reckoned as one of the four heads of the Leopard. It is a mistake, however, to allocate two heads to the Bear, despite the fact that the Medo-Persian Empire is represented by a Ram with two horns (Dan. 8:3). Not every horn of the Ram and He-Goat is represented by one of the heads of the Beast. This is evident from the fact that the great horn of the He-Goat which represents Alexander the Great is not represented by any one head of the Beast (but instead by the four heads of the Leopard). The seven heads of the Beast represent the seven heads of the four beasts that rise up from the sea in Daniel chapter 7, not the horns of chapter 8. The Bear (the Medo-Persian Empire) is clearly represented with only one head, for the Bear only has one mouth (Dan. 7:5).

The seventh kingdom represented by the seventh head of the Beast is to **remain only a little while** (Rev. 17:10). The former USSR which was indeed short-lived.

Printed in Great Britain
by Amazon

56578328R00020